Copyright 2020 - by Beth Costanzo

Crabs are some of the most interesting creatures on our planet today. It's easy to be scared (when you look at one of them. Their pincers are scary and they can really hurt if they decide to pinch you!

But getting beyond that fear, the crab has many fascinating things going on. By taking the time to appreciate them, you may even find that the crab is one of your favorite animals!

Fun Facts About Crabs

Crabs are some seriously old creatures. They trace their origins back to the Jurassic era. Because of this, there are around 850 different types of crabs. They can include everything from saltwater crabs and freshwater crabs to brackish water crabs. These types of crabs can be found in many different locations around the world. Often, you can see these crabs in tropical regions.

From there, let's talk about the crab's physical appearance. Like we discussed in the beginning, one of the most notable features of a crab is its single pair of pincers. It basically has two functions. First, crabs use their pincers to fend off predators. If a larger fish or other animal is preparing to eat the crab, the crab can use these pincers to fight back. Crabs also have thick exoskeletons, which protect them from some of the hungriest predators in the sea.

Besides protecting itself, the crab can also gather food with its pincers. Crabs tend to eat both plants and other animals. In terms of plants, crabs love to munch on things like plankton, algae, and even fungi. As for animals, crabs will really eat anything that they can get, which often includes the carcasses of dead fish.

If you were to see a crab in the wild, you'll likely notice that it tends to walk sideways. This is because of how the crab's legs are created. Basically, crabs walk sideways because it is more efficient for them to do so. You may also sometimes notice that crabs tend to attack each other. Ultimately, crabs are an aggressive species. Male crabs often fight each other in order to gain the attention of female crabs. In other situations, they may be fighting because they are trying to protect their shelter.

Like many other animals, crabs are enjoyed by humans. In fact, crabs total around 20% of marine crustacean animals that are farmed consumed. You may have even eaten crabs before. Humans love eating crab legs and crab claws. While it may take some time to crack them, they can be delicious.

Unlike other animals, crabs aren't endangered at this point. However, it is always important to be careful of the overfishing and overconsumption of this animal. If we aren't careful, it could disappear from our planet for good.

Appreciating This Interesting Creature

In sum, the crab is a small, yet complex creature. It is aggressive and uses its noticeable pinches to protect itself. Whether you spot one when you are swimming or are looking to enjoy one for your next meal, I hope that you've come to appreciate this fascinating animal.

CRAB ACTIVITIES

TRACING

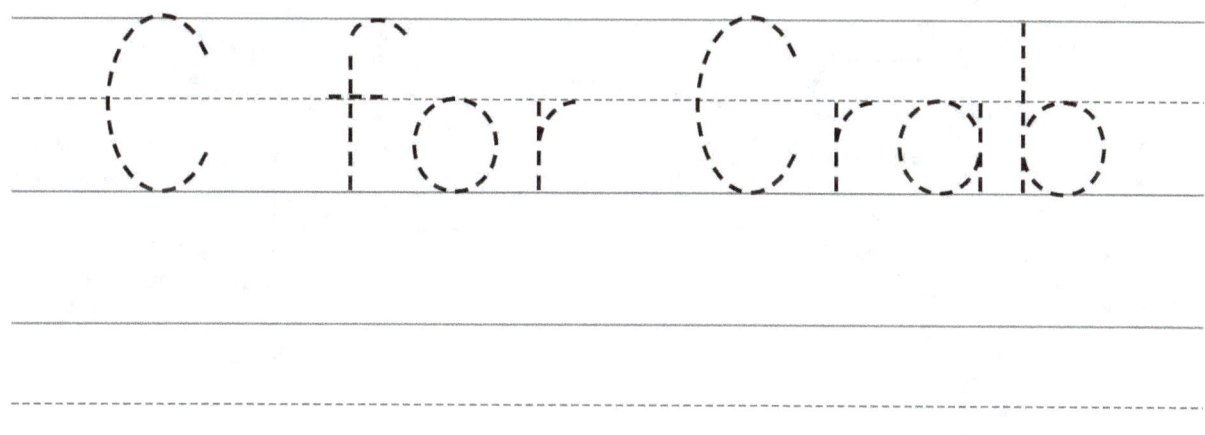

COLORING

Color the crab.

BODY PARTS

Write the name of the body parts of the crab in the correct place.

Eye | Leg | Carapace | Claw | Shell

COUNTING

Count the Crabs then circle the correct answer.

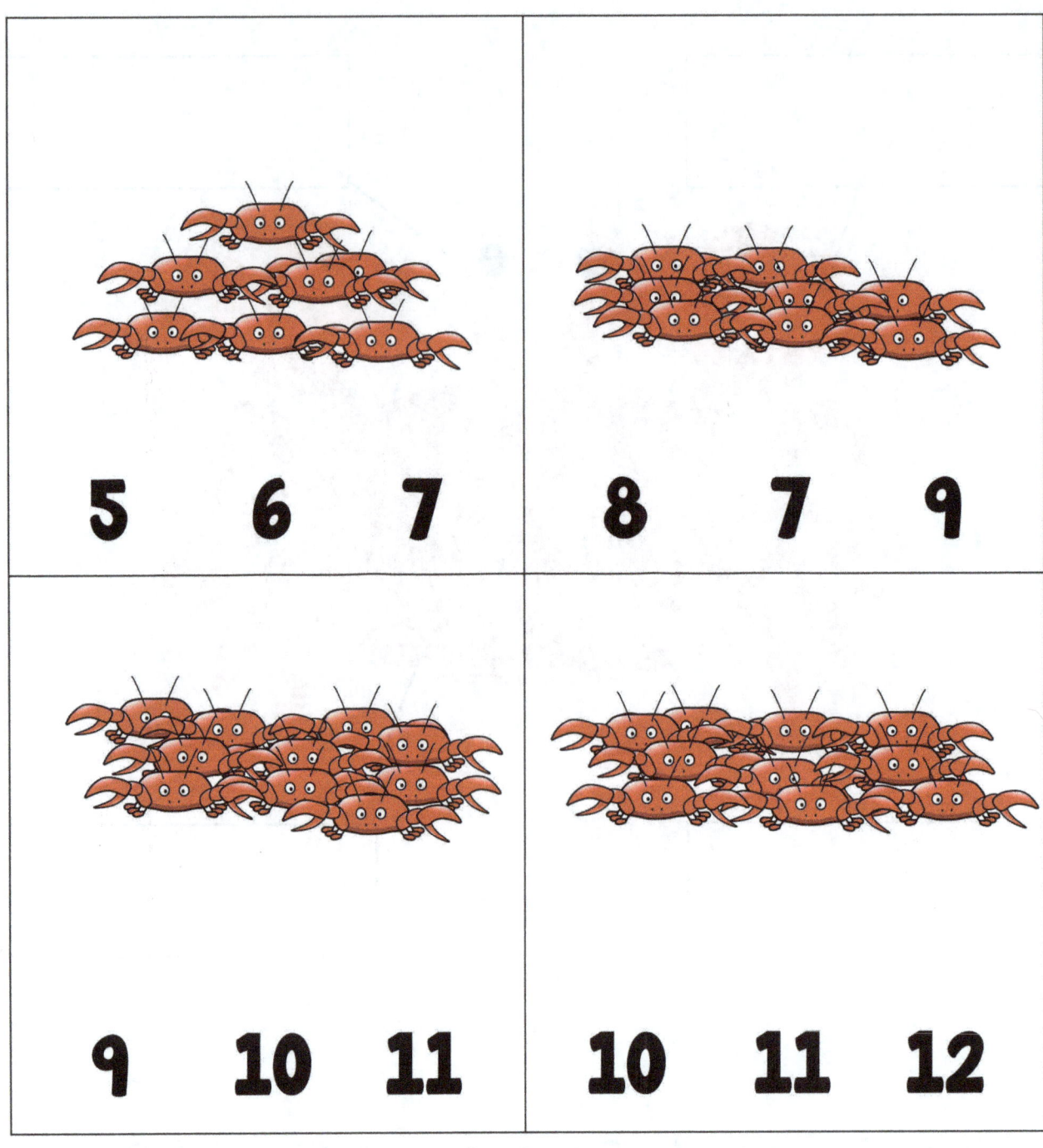

CONNECT THE DOTS

COUNT AND GRAPH

MATCH THE COLORS

COUNT AND WRITE THE MISSING NUMBERS

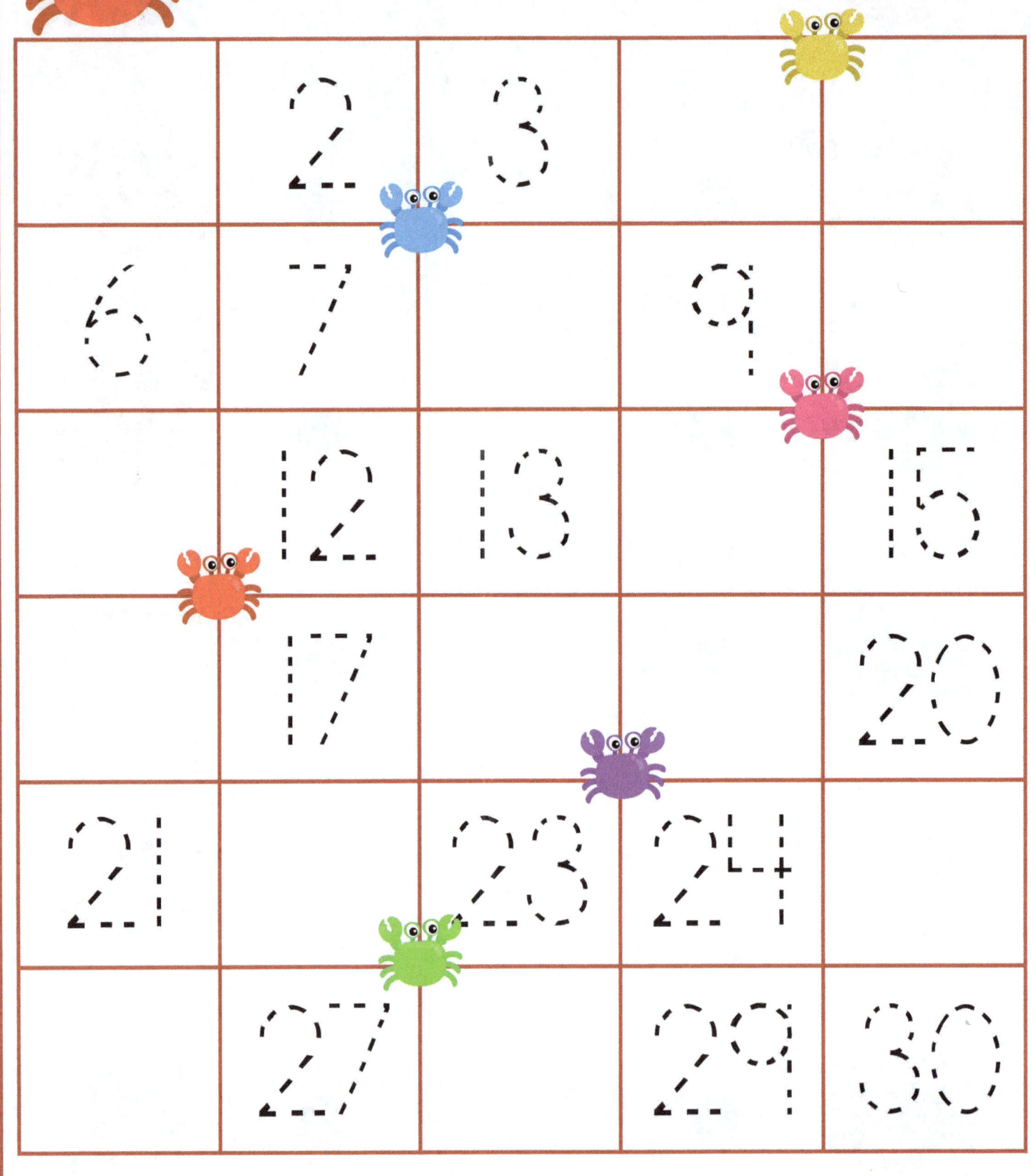

WHAT COMES NEXT?

CRAB HEADBAND CRAFT

Cut and glue the pieces to make a crab headband!

Visit us at:

www.adventuresofscubajack.com

www.ingramcontent.com/pod-product-compliance
Lightning Source LLC
Chambersburg PA
CBHW060429010526

44118CB00017B/2421